WHSmith

Revise

English

KS3: YEAR 7
Book 2

Age 11–12

Roger Machin

First published in 2007
exclusively for WHSmith by
Hodder Education, an Hachette UK company
338 Euston Road
London
NW1 3BH

Impression number   10 9 8 7 6 5 4 3 2
Year   2011 2010 2009
Text © Hodder Education 2007

All text extracts written by the author, unless otherwise acknowledged.

A CIP record for this book is available from the British Library.

Cover illustration by Sally Newton Illustrations

Typeset by GreenGate Publishing Services, Tonbridge, Kent

ISBN: 978 0 340 94294 9

Printed and bound in Spain.

Contents

How to use this book

The fact that you are choosing to read these words means you are thinking about improving your English. Congratulations! This is the first step towards success and you have taken it already. Your desire to succeed is the essential ingredient to progress. Think of this book as your partner, your personal trainer, in your quest to achieve.

Key Stage 3

Key Stage 3 (you'll often see it called just KS3) is the name given to Years 7, 8 and 9. Students in KS3 are normally aged between 11 and 14 years old. It is a crucial time for all subjects and no less so for English. It is the time when the lessons learned from junior school are built upon and when the foundations are laid for study up to GCSE. Almost all students do the compulsory KS3 test at the end of Year 9. Many schools now opt to take similar tests at the end of Years 7 and 8.

English at KS3

The English tests at KS3 assess students in two basic areas: their ability to read and write. Teachers assess the other two components of English (speaking and listening) separately. Students are expected to read lots of different sorts of texts (for example, stories, newspapers, biographies) and to show their understanding of them. They are expected to demonstrate that they can write in a variety of ways (for example, imaginatively, persuasively, informatively) and in good English. This book, along with the other five books in this series, covers every single one of the skills you need to achieve the best you possibly can in the English tests.

Revision

Many students think of revision as something they do just before a test takes place. Don't be one of them! Success is based on continual revision, just a little every day. Go over what you know. Check, recheck and identify areas of difficulty. Practise what you're good at and get help in areas where you're weaker. Let this book be your friend and companion in this process. An exercise every day or two – more if you're enjoying yourself – will be enough to build up your confidence and ability. Successful revision is like effective physical training: it needs to be gradual.

The *Revise KS3 English* family

This book is one of a family of six books designed to improve your performance in English at KS3. There are two books for each year group and 26 units in each book. Each unit focuses on one of the skills you will need to learn or revise as you progress from Year 7 through to Year 9. Once you feel confident in the skills revised in the Year 7 books you can move on up to Year 8. It doesn't matter which year group you are actually in. Neither does it matter if you are in Year 9 and you want to use the Year 7 books as kick-starters. Use the books that you feel comfortable with and go with your instincts.

Using this book

Work through the units in the order they appear. In other words, start with Unit 1 and finish with Unit 26. The reason for this is that the skills learned and revised earlier in the book are built upon as the text progresses. There is no fixed time limit for each unit although you should be able to finish most of them in a single sitting. Towards the end of each of the units you will find a more challenging section (shaded in mauve). This section is designed to help you push yourself that little bit further in the direction of understanding and success. The Revision booster boxes and Revision tips at the side also help with your study.

Home study tips

You'll discover fairly quickly that the answers are at the end of the book! Try not to look at them until you have worked as hard as you possibly can on the unit. The fact that you are working at home means you are eager to improve and to get ahead. You're not going to do this if you take the easy way out. Engage with what you read, and write answers as fully and in as much detail as you can. Remember that you are taking responsibility for your own learning. Not many students do this and if you do it properly it is going to give you an advantage.

If you work steadily through this book and the other books in the series your English will improve. This is a definite, cast-iron and unarguable fact. It might seem hard at first, especially if you're tired after a long day's work. But stick with it. Mental stamina, just like physical stamina, improves with exercise. Don't get downhearted if you can't complete an exercise. Give it your best shot and if you're still stuck in a rut, move on to another unit. Remember that the best way to get ahead is to get started and you're about to get started right now!

1: Prepositions

In this unit you will learn
- to use prepositions in phrases

Get started

Nouns are the names of people, places, things and ideas. You may not be able to *touch* or *feel* a noun in the real world. Often, however, you can tell whether a word is a noun by putting it after the word *the,* and seeing whether it makes sense. For example

the truth and *the robot* are phrases that make sense.

the next and *the friendly* don't make sense without adding extra words.

Using this test you can see that *truth* and *robot* are nouns.

Practice

1 Identify the nouns in the following list. Test the words with *the* if you need to.

monkey   are   sadness   apple   beyond   story   furious   suddenly   as invitation

The word *the* is called a **determiner**. It is one of a group of words that goes directly before a noun to show how the noun is being used. In other words, it *determines* the use of the noun. Common determiners are

the   some   a   many   our   their   this   that   his   these   my   every

2 Locate six determiners in the following sentences.

A fish swam silently through the pond.

Every car driving down that bus lane was stopped.

Some people lost their money.

Prepositions are words that go before nouns (or nouns and determiners) to make phrases like these.

in a mess ✓

on time ✓

with every minute ✓

over this mountain ✓

under some books ✓

at home

3 a Write down the six prepositions in the phrases on the left.

  b List the four determiners that have been used.

The phrases on the left do not contain **verbs** (*action* or *doing* words) and writers would not normally use them as complete sentences. There needs to be something happening within the sentence to give it meaning. This can be done by adding a subject and a verb.

The girl's hair was in a mess.

The phrase *in a mess* is used to describe *the girl's hair.* The whole thing together creates a sentence that makes complete sense on its own.

4 Choose one of the following to add to each of the other five phrases on the left. When you have finished, you should have five complete sentences, each of which makes sense.

The Queen never seems to be

A dangerous troll is said to live

The train from Leeds is

This rare beetle was unfortunately squashed

I think more about you

The phrases that start with prepositions are called **adverbial phrases** if they describe **how** or **when** something happens.

*The captain shouted at her team **in a fury**.*

*The water was reduced to a dribble **in a few moments**.*

You can then create variety and effect by choosing sometimes to move your adverbial phrase to the start of a sentence.

In a fury, the captain shouted at her team.

In a few moments, the water was reduced to a dribble.

 Phrases that start with prepositions can often be moved around within sentences to create good effects.

5 Change the following sentences to place the adverbial phrase at the start of each. Notice from the examples that each phrase must be sectioned off with a comma.

We have five minutes at most.

She collapsed completely under the terrible pressure.

How did I do?

I know how to use prepositions in phrases.

2: Writing description

Get started

Anyone who writes imaginatively has to balance description with action. In the following passage, the first sentence is descriptive and the second refers to an action.

The old man sat in the corner of the room. The telephone rang and the old man went to answer it.

The first sentence describes the old man. The second sentence relates to his actions when the telephone rings.

Practice

1 State whether each of the following sentences relates to a description or an action.

a *The little girl was dressed in red.*

b *The boy leapt into the pond.*

c *The bird was large and clumsy.*

d *All was still and the factory lay deserted.*

e *Everyone screamed and shouted as the ride began.*

In practice, of course, description and action are often presented in one and the same sentence.

The little girl with red hair leapt into the pond.

It is very common, however, for students to concentrate far too much on action when they write imaginatively. If the focus is too much on action, then this is the sort of text that can result.

The old man sat in the corner of the room. The telephone rang and the old man went to answer it. He spoke for a while and then put the phone down. He opened the door and walked out. He went down the street as fast as he could. He stopped at the bus stop. A bus came and he got on. He went to the middle of town.

Imaginative writing is much more interesting if it contains more description than the text above. Good description is worth lots of marks in well-written fiction.

The lonely old man sat in the corner of the room. His bleary eyes looked sadly out into the gloom. His face was a cobweb of wrinkles. Outside, the rain fell steadily. It ran down the window pane like tears down unhappy cheeks. In the distance, a telephone rang. The old man rose slowly, painfully from his chair.

The second passage about the old man is far more *descriptive.* The reader is given a much better sense of the feeling that surrounds the old man and his setting. The writer has created a much more interesting text using just a few simple techniques.

2

a The opening sentences of both passages are identical but for one word. Which one?

b What adjective is used in the second sentence to describe the old man's eyes?

c Which adverb describes the way the man's eyes are looking out?

d What noun describes where the man is looking?

e What impression do you get of the old man and his surroundings in the opening two sentences?

Recall that adverbs are used mainly to describe and give detail to verbs. The adverb you've identified in **2c** above describes (or modifies) the verb *looked.*

3

a What adverb is used to modify the verb *fell*?

b How is the rain made to seem more gloomy with this adverb?

Sometimes adverbs are used in pairs, to emphasise the intended effect.

The rain fell relentlessly, constantly.

4

Which adverbs in the text does the writer use for this descriptive technique?

Revision booster

Similes and metaphors are excellent ways of adding depth to a description. The writer of the second passage has used both. Remember that similes and metaphors are used to create comparisons between one thing and another. They create a picture (an *image*) in the mind of the reader.

5

What is the old man's face compared to?

A simile is a comparison introduced with the word *like* or *as.*

6

What two things in the passage are compared with a simile?

(!) Simple techniques used well can add great depth to descriptions. This unit has looked at the way adverbs, adjectives, similes and metaphors can be used carefully for this purpose.

How did I do?

I can consider descriptive techniques.   ✔

3: Verb forms

In this unit you will learn
- ▸ to work with different verb forms

Get started

Verbs are words that refer to actions or states.

*She **kicked** the ball.*   *They **auctioned** the statue.*   *Kurtis **seems** unhappy.*

The first two verbs refer to the *actions* of kicking and auctioning. The third verb refers to the *state* of seeming to be something.

Practice

1 Identify the (single-word) verbs in each of the following sentences.

Davinia locked the door.

Alberto brings home fish every day.

She appears not to care.

I often think about it.

They smashed into each other on the ice rink.

Verbs change their form according to certain fixed rules. The infinitive form is used after the preposition *to*.

to laugh   to cry   to fall   to grow   to seem

It makes no sense to say *to locked,* so you know that *locked* is not the infinitive form.

2 Put each of the five verbs from question 1 into the infinitive form.

Verbs also change their form according to the tense they are in.

I try   is a present tense form

I tried   is a past tense form

I will try   is a future tense form

3 Put the following verbs into the present, past and future tenses. Use the pronoun *I* as in the examples.

go   bring   have   begin

Although English has different tenses to indicate different times (past, present and future) these divisions are not at all rigid. It is possible to say, for example,

I fly to Paris tomorrow morning.

This is obviously the present tense (of the verb *fly*) to refer to something that is going to happen in the future. This is not uncommon. You have also probably read or heard something like this.

Their boy dives and the ref gives a penalty. We weren't going to win after that.

In this case, the verbs *dives* and *gives* are used in the present tense to refer to something that happened in the past.

Remember that the expressions *past*, *present* and *future* are general descriptions of the uses of verb tense. You need to look at the context (how and where the verb is being used) to understand exactly what time is being referred to in each case.

The word *will* is used before the infinitive form of a main verb to create the future tense. Other modal verbs alter or modify the meanings of main verbs in different ways. Modal verbs are typically placed before the verb they modify.

can   will   might   should   could   must   may   would

4 Identify the modal verbs and the main verbs in each of the following sentences.

In a few days they will come to Dublin.

A few words might help.

I can see what's wrong.

Sally could buy herself a ticket.

Martin would wait outside every night without fail.

The verb *will* is an example of a **modal verb**. Modal verbs are followed by the infinitive form of a main verb.

Revision booster

Look again at the list of eight modal verbs above. Use each of them in turn before the main verb *enjoy* in the following sentence. Notice how the meaning of the sentence is modified slightly on each occasion.
I enjoy myself.

How did I do?

I can work with different verb forms.   ✔ ☐

4: Point of view

In this unit you will learn
- to interpret point of view

Get started

This extract from an article about stage schools appeared recently in a national newspaper. The author is a journalist called Penny Boynton.

> Stage schools have been around for many years now. In their early days, they catered only for children of the well to do. They were really no more than finishing schools where wealthy children were sent to have their speech and deportment refined. The rich kids who went to these places could afford to waste their time prancing around in leggings and polishing their vowels. Stage schools turned spoilt brats into unbearably spoilt brats.

Look carefully at the nouns and noun phrases used by a writer throughout a piece of writing. They will often tell you lots about the way a writer feels towards a subject. In this article, for instance, Penny Boynton describes the basic noun phrase *stage schools* in the following ways.

Stage schools   they   They   finishing schools   these places   Stage schools

These nouns are called a **reference chain**. In other words, all the nouns, pronouns and noun phrases in the chain refer to the same thing. Reference chains hold texts together (without endless repetitions of the same nouns or pronouns like *they*) and they give a reader clues about writer attitude. In this case, the writer's attitude towards *finishing schools* and *these places* does not seem very positive.

Practice

1 a Make your own reference chain of noun phrases (just noun phrases this time) that are used to refer to the children who used to go to stage school. You should find five phrases to make up your chain.

   b What does your reference chain suggest to you about Penny Boynton's feelings towards the children she describes?

   c What is your own reaction to the author's opinions?

2 Look at the author's choice of the verbs *prancing* and *polishing.* What do these verbs suggest about the children at stage school?

3 The author makes it clear early on in the passage that she is not talking about stage schools as they are now. Write down the four-word phrase (beginning with a preposition) that makes it clear she is talking about the past.

Remember that adverbial phrases can move around in sentences. The phrase you identified in question 3 has been used at the start of a sentence to provide variety.

④ a Rewrite the second sentence by moving the adverbial phrase to the end.

    b Now reread the first three sentences of the extract. What did the writer avoid by putting an adverbial phrase at the start of the second sentence?

Penny Boynton's article continues a little later in the following way.

> Stage schools have now changed. They are centres of excellence where children from all backgrounds can work together on constructive and stimulating projects. They provide excellent training for every child.

⑤ Which single adverb, used in the first sentence, provides a contrast with the *early days*?

Revision booster

⑥ a Make a reference chain for the stage schools in this passage. It should contain two pronouns and two noun phrases.

    b How has the writer changed the way she describes stage schools?

⑦ Find three adjectives (two that describe *projects* and one that describes *training*) that demonstrate the writer's change in attitude.

⑧ Look at the determiners used before the nouns *backgrounds* and *child*. How do these determiners emphasise the difference (in the writer's eyes) between stage schools now and in the past?

How did I do?

I can interpret point of view.   ✔
                                                                      ☐

5: Participles

In this unit you will learn
▷ to explore the functions of participles

Get started

You already know that verbs change their forms in order to indicate when actions take place.

I follow   is the present tense
I followed   is the past tense
I will follow   is the future tense

There are other kinds of time, however, that can also be indicated with verb tense. First of all, there are the *perfect* tenses. These are formed by using a form of the verb *have* in front of the **perfect** (or **past**) **participle**.

*Ashok **has made** his lunch.*   (*present* perfect tense)
*Callum **had brought** a picnic.*   (*past* perfect tense)

The **present perfect** is formed with *has/have* and the perfect participle.

The **past perfect** is formed with *had* and the perfect participle.

To work out the perfect participle, take the infinitive of the main verb and put the word *have* before it. Change the form of the verb until it makes sense. You then have the perfect participle. For example

have see and *have go* do not make sense.
have seen and *have gone* do make sense.

So the perfect participles of *see* and *go* are *seen* and *gone.*

Practice

1 What are the perfect participles of the following verbs?

   talk   think   buy   grow   swim

2 Now turn each of the following present tense sentences into

   a the present perfect tense

   b the past perfect tense

   I think about it.
   She does very well.
   They make up their minds.

The perfect tenses are often used to show that an action is just completed and a new action is about to begin. For example

She has done her homework and now she wants to go out.
He had thought long and hard but decided against it.

The second kind of verb tenses looked at in this unit are the **continuous tenses**. These are made by creating the **continuous** (also called **progressive**) **participle** and adding it to a form of the verb *be.* The continuous participle is easy to identify. It is the root of the verb added to the suffix *ing.* Examples of the **continuous participle** are

doing   being   eating   laughing   crossing

Here are some examples of the **present continuous** tense.

I am doing absolutely nothing.
She is smashing atoms in the laboratory.

Here are some examples of the **past continuous** tense (using a past form of the verb *be*).

They were arguing for years.
I was biting my lip.

Different verb tenses are often used in the same sentence.

3 For each of the following, change the underlined verbs in the sentences on the left to the tenses given in brackets on the right. The first one is done for you.

*I **walk** to school when I **see** the fire.*   (past continuous and simple past)

I was walking to school when I saw the fire.

*I **bring** my coat in case it **rains**.*   (past perfect and simple past)

*The baby **cries** because he **hurts** himself.*   (present continuous and present perfect)

*He was **wash** up before she **finish**.*   (past continuous and past perfect)

Revision booster

The perfect participle can often be used as an adjective. For example
He returned to the village, a broken man.
Broken is the perfect participle of the verb *break.*

4 Make an adjective from the perfect participle of the verb given in brackets in each of the following sentences.
He walked into the (cramp) cell.
A (fall) idol, he stared bitterly at his future.
This is a (try) and (test) formula.
The cloth was like (spin) gold.

How did I do?

✔
I can explore the functions of participles.   ☐

6: Fact and opinion

In this unit you will learn
▶ to present information

Get started

A school near Plymouth recently arranged an Open Day for the parents and carers of Year 7 pupils. A student from Year 7 called Tim Harris was asked to write a letter home to provide information about the day.

You may already know that the Year 7 Open Day will be taking place on Tuesday, 6th April. It is intended as an opportunity for parents and carers to come into the school and actually see what their children do on a daily basis. There will be exhibitions of students' work, demonstrations of activities and chances for parents to become involved in a variety of events. The day will begin with an introduction from Mrs Cooke at 9.30 in Room P4. Parents are welcome to stay for as long or as short a time as they wish. We do hope you will be able to attend. It's going to be an excellent day.

Practice

Informative writing must contain useful facts.

1 a Which two hard facts does Tim Harris provide in this letter about date and time?

b What fact does Tim provide about where the Open Day will start off?

Opinions can often provide interest to informative writing.

2 Tim offers an opinion at the end of his letter. What kind of day does he believe people will have?

There are two important ways of expressing uncertainty in language. One way, of course, is by asking a direct question.

Did you know I have your credit card?

The other way is by using one of the modal verbs you've worked with in previous units. Modal verbs are often used to *suggest*. They are *less direct* than questions and they are often used in formal writing.

You may know I have your credit card.

Modal verbs express uncertainty. They can be used in texts to do this either with or instead of direct questions.

3 In which sentence does Tim use a modal verb in the way shown here?

Writers base their information around nouns. After all, it is *things* that readers of the information need to know about. Nouns can obviously provide information on their own (or with a single determiner like *a*). For example

a display

a presentation

but these nouns can be given detail and depth by using prepositions to expand them into longer noun phrases.

a display of colour

a presentation of dances from around the world

activities for everyone

Tim Harris used the prepositions *of, for* and *from* in a variety of noun phrases. One of his noun phrases is

opportunity for parents

④ Find three other noun phrases like the one above in the letter.

You have already looked at the way modal verbs can be used to express uncertainty. The verb *do* can be placed in front of an infinitive (just as a modal verb is) to express not uncertainty but emphasis.

*I **do** want to go.   Those shoes **do** look fantastic.   They **do** regret their actions.*

⑤ a Write down the sentence in the text where Tim Harris does this.

b How is he trying to make his audience feel?

Tim Harris is describing a future event (the Open Day) so it is not surprising that he often uses the simple future tense in his letter. In other words, he places *will* before an infinitive form to make combinations like *will be* and *will begin*. The future, however, can be expressed in other ways. One of them is by taking the continuous participle (*ing* form) of *go* and adding it to the preposition *to* and an infinitive.

going to dance   going to make   going to build

⑥ Write down the sentence in which Tim Harris expresses future time in this way.

How did I do?

I can present information.   ☐

7: Using connectives

In this unit you will learn
▌ to connect simple sentences

Get started

A **simple sentence** contains a single verb. The verb is normally attached to a noun or pronoun that it is *about.*

Paula combed her hair.

The verb is *combed* and the person who does the combing is Paula. The sentence is *about* Paula so it is said that Paula is the **subject** of the sentence. The subject sometimes *does something* to another noun. In this case, Paula combed *her hair.* Her hair is the thing which has had something done to it and it is said to be the **object** of the sentence.

A simple sentence might contain just a verb.

Stop!   Wait!   Run!

It can contain a verb and an object.

Take that!   Bring water.   Stay calm.

It could contain a subject and a verb.

Paula drives.   He rollerblades.   Harry flies.

Or it can contain a subject, a verb and an object.

Paula drives buses.   Isadora eats pilchards.   I love it.

Practice

1 In the following simple sentences, identify the

a three subjects

b five verbs

c four objects

Think!   Arun made tea.   Harry flies planes.   Have fun.   I collect fossils.

Simple sentences are certainly grammatical. If they are overused, however, they will make writing dull.

Look at the following two simple sentences.

Alana left school. She started a business.

These are two perfectly grammatical sentences. They contain two subjects (*Alana* and *She*), two verbs (*left* and *started*) and two objects (*school* and *a business*). You can probably see, though, that too many sentences like this will very soon send a reader to sleep. These sorts of sentences are fine once or twice in a text to add variety. On the whole, however, simple sentences need to be developed into sentences with more than one verb.

The easiest way of doing this is to insert a **connective** like *and.*

*Alana left school **and** she started a business.*

Other words used as connectives are

but   when   if   because   while   until   unless   since   as   although

2 Using a different connective each time, link each of the following pairs of simple sentences.

Sid cooks dinner. His mum does it for him.

He makes the toast. His eggs are boiling.

He washes up. Nobody else will do it for him.

He cleans his teeth. He watches the television.

Simple sentences can also be connected by using **participles**. Participles, remember, are verb forms that can follow *has* and *is.* For example

ridden   smiled   done   brought   gone   (perfect participle)

riding   smiling   doing   bringing   going   (continuous participle)

Here are two simple sentences.

Robin Hood rode to Nottingham. He prepared for the fight.

They can be linked with the word *having* plus the perfect participle.

Having ridden to Nottingham, Robin Hood prepared for the fight.

Or the word *after* plus the continuous participle.

After riding to Nottingham, Robin Hood prepared for the fight.

3 Using the sentences about Robin Hood as your guide, link these three pairs of simple sentences using the

a perfect participles

b continuous participles

The president waved to the crowds. He returned to his office.

He beat the egg. He poured it into the mixer.

Kirsty spoke to the press. She went back to her hotel.

How did I do?

I can connect simple sentences.

✔

8: Literary writing

In this unit you will learn
- to analyse literary writing

Read the following passage. It is an account taken from a book about childhood in Ireland in the 1930s. It describes a playground bully called Donleavy who picks on a smaller boy called Farrell.

I could see Donleavy sitting on a drain chewing a blade of grass. He looked completely relaxed. As usual, he was surrounded by two or three hangers on, the chaps who laughed loudest at all his nasty jokes.

Donleavy had spotted Farrell in his brother's old shorts, two sizes too big. Farrell sidled round the edge of the toilets as he always did when Donleavy was around, but Donleavy wasn't going to let him escape.

'Farrell,' called Donleavy, with mock politeness. 'You have the wrong shorts.'

Farrell froze. 'Get lost, Donleavy,' he replied. 'I'm not talking to you.'

This response, which must have taken all of Farrell's courage, caused Donleavy's parasites to raise their eyebrows and gawp at each other as if mortally offended on their leader's behalf.

Donleavy raised himself from his seat and walked calmly over to Farrell.

'Now, Farrell,' he said with great patience. 'I have tried to be civil to you and you continually respond with rudeness.' He sighed and shook his head as if in great sadness. 'If civility fails then punishment must follow.'

With a sudden movement, Donleavy grabbed Farrell's hair and wrenched him through the open toilet door.

Practice

The way characters are introduced has a significant impact on how readers respond to them.

1 In no more than two sentences, contrast the reader's first impressions of Donleavy and Farrell.

2 a When Donleavy tells Farrell his shorts are too big, how does he do it?

   b Farrell doesn't want to go along with the game. How does he respond to Donleavy?

   c How do Donleavy's friends continue the game at Farrell's expense?

Donleavy continues to play around with Farrell's emotions as the passage develops.

3 a How does Donleavy talk to Farrell when he first walks over to him?

b How does Donleavy pretend that punishing Farrell will make him feel?

The writer (or narrator) of this piece clearly has contempt for Donleavy's friends.

4 Write down two noun references that demonstrate the narrator's feelings towards Donleavy's friends.

In the first paragraph, there is evidence that Donleavy's friends are anxious to prove they like him.

5 a What do Donleavy's friends always do that shows this?

b What is the narrator's attitude towards Donleavy's jokes?

This story has a narrator who is part of the action. In this particular passage, the narrator is not playing an active role. You can, however, sense the nature of some of his thoughts and feelings.

The verbs chosen by writers can have a dramatic impact on a reader's understanding of a text. In this extract, for example, the verbs chosen to describe the way Farrell moves and stops are important in creating a sense of his terror in the face of the bully.

6 a Which verb is used to describe Farrell's movements at the start of the passage?

b Which verb is used to describe the way Farrell stops after Donleavy calls out?

Revision booster

Verbs are also important in providing dramatic contrasts.

Throughout the passage, Donleavy is described as calm and patient and even sad. This account hides the fact, of course, that Donleavy is only pretending to treat Farrell with concern in order to make his bullying more fun.

7 Which two verbs, used at the end of the passage, show Donleavy as he really is?

How did I do?

I can analyse literary writing.

✔
☐

9: Foregrounds in sentences

In this unit you will learn
- ▶ to foreground for variety

Get started

Remember that simple sentences are those that contain just a single verb. Here is a string of three simple sentences.

Saul strode to the force field. He put out his hand. He disappeared in an instant.

This piece of writing is grammatically correct but it is dull. One way of adding variety is by altering the sentence structure. The sentence structure can be altered by something called **foregrounding**. Writers foreground when they put something unexpected at the beginning of a sentence. For example, the three sentences above all start with *Saul* or *He.* To add variety you could foreground the adverbial phrase at the end of the third sentence. The adverbial phrase is *in an instant.*

Saul strode to the force field. He put out his hand. In an instant, he disappeared.

This is an improvement on the original. Notice that the foregrounded adverbial phrase is separated from the rest of the sentence by a comma.

> ⊘ Words, phrases and clauses can all be foregrounded. They are normally separated from the rest of their sentences by a comma.

Practice

1 The three sentences below all contain adverbial phrases. Rewrite them so that the phrases are foregrounded. Do not forget to include the comma.

He'll be coming in a second.

She strode off in a fury.

He lay down silently on a lonely hilltop.

Single-word adverbs can also be effective in a foregrounded position.

Angrily, Saul strode to the force field.

2 Add single adverbs as foregrounds to the following sentences. Remember the comma.

They parted for the last time.

The children ran into the fairground.

A complex sentence contains two or more verbs. Clauses are those parts of complex sentences that contain verbs. For example, the sentence

Saul strode to the force field as the humming grew louder.

contains two clauses based on the verbs *strode* and *grew.*

Saul strode to the force field

the humming grew louder

Notice that these two clauses could form two separate simple sentences with one verb each. The two clauses in the complex sentence are joined by the connective *as*. The second clause can be foregrounded to create variety in just the same way as you foregrounded the adverbial phrases and the single adverbs.

As the humming grew louder, Saul strode towards the force field.

3 Foreground the second clause in each of the following three sentences. Again, don't forget to include the comma.

I'm going to lose my temper if you don't stop messing around.

It was a real problem when she found out.

Take care until the next time.

Participle phrases can also be foregrounded as in the following examples.

Saul shuffled towards the force field, grumbling irritably.

Grumbling irritably, Saul shuffled towards the force field.

4 Foreground the participle phrases in these sentences. These already need commas, to make the phrase refer to the subject of the sentence.

He watched the film, laughing all the time.

The baby woke me, crying loudly.

She prepared her performance, breathing deeply.

Revision booster

Using the techniques learned in this unit, the original three sentences could be reformed in a much more interesting way.

Looking determined, Saul strode to the force field. Bravely, he put out his hand. In an instant, he disappeared.

5 What different features have been foregrounded in each of these three sentences?

How did I do?

I can foreground for variety.

10: Features of narrative

Get started

The following extract is from the start of a group diary. It was written by Year 7 students on their return from a weekend hiking in the Yorkshire Wolds.

> We woke up early. Tent 3 had collapsed during the night and its inhabitants (Jessica and Minette) were using it as a duvet. Mr Walters was already cooking breakfast in a far corner of the field but he seemed unhappy. After a while we could see why. The sausages were stuck to the bottom of the pan because, as Mr Walters insisted, our school's portable gas cooker was 'out of date'. We believed you, Mr Walters. In the end we all had toast and nobody minded at all.

Narrative writing typically progresses in a way that can easily be followed by the reader. This diary account was intended to be read by students, parents and others who would not necessarily have any background information about the events described. It needed to be clear and well organised.

An important way of organising this sort of narrative is through the use of adverbs and adverbial phrases that relate to time. These words and phrases include

next   now   after a while   during the night   in the end   already   later   early

Words and phrases like this are crucial in organising events in a reader's mind. They show progression from one thing to another.

Practice

1 Five of the eight adverbs/adverbial phrases in the list above can be found in the diary extract. Which are they?

Reread the passage but take out the adverbs and adverbial phrases you located. Notice how the extract loses its sense of time structure.

Adverbial phrases can often be replaced by single adverbs. For example

at the current time	can become	*currently*
all of a sudden	can become	*suddenly*
in an instant	can become	*instantly*

2 Look at the last adverbial phrase you picked out in question 1. What single adverb could replace it?

This sort of narrative is designed to be interesting to a wide range of readers. One of the ways of making a report or a diary account interesting is to include anecdotes. **Anecdotes** are short stories, often amusing, that people recall as experiences.

3 This extract has two anecdotes. What are the two separate anecdotes described by the students in their account?

Neither anecdote would be funny if it wasn't for the reactions of those involved.

4 a How is the first anecdote made amusing by what the girls do?

b How is the second anecdote made funny by the teacher's response?

Inverted commas are often used to show that something is to be questioned. For example

He said he was 'busy working late' but I wasn't sure what he was up to.

They said they were 'in an important meeting' but I had my own ideas about that.

5 a Write down the section in the passage that is enclosed by inverted commas.

b The students clearly don't believe what's in the inverted commas. What do you think they do believe?

The passage continues after the inverted commas in a teasing sort of way.

6 Write down a complete sentence that is obviously used to tease Mr Walters.

The anecdote about Mr Walters is an example of very gentle **irony**. At no point do the students say exactly what they think about the burnt sausages. They just suggest it through the inverted commas. In their teasing sentence they actually say the *opposite* of what they believe and yet the reader still gets the point they are making.

7 The irony comes to an end with a four-word phrase. The phrase makes it clear that the loss of the sausages didn't *really* matter to anyone. What is it?

How did I do?

I can explore features of narrative.

11: Using adjectives

In this unit you will learn
  ▶ to include adjectives in noun phrases

Get started

Recall that a noun phrase is made up of at least a single noun like *ideas*. It may be attached to a determiner like this: ***the*** *ideas.* In addition, it can include an adjective: *the **crazy** ideas.*

A proposal was recently made to build a road through a park in south east England. A pressure group was set up to resist the proposals. This extract is from the end of a letter that the group sent to local people.

The people are angry and frustrated. This absurd proposal should never have been made. Our magnificent park with its wonderful trees must not disappear.

Remember that adjectives are words used to describe nouns. This extract uses adjectives to describe the people, the proposal and the park.

Practice

1 Complete the following sentences. You should end up using five adjectives in total.

The people are ...

The proposal is ...

The park (and its trees) are ...

Notice how the adjectives are used to create a very different picture of each noun.

Adjectives can be used before the noun they modify.

*The **injured** beast*   *The **stale** bread*

Or they can be used after the noun and a verb of state like *be, go* or *seem.*

*The beast seems **injured**.*   *The bread has gone **stale**.*

2 Of the three nouns in the passage, which one is modified by adjectives that follow it?

3 Locate the adjectives in each of the following sentences. Then place them *before* the noun they describe to create three new noun phrases.

The night had become grim and dark.

The volcano appeared quiet.

The curry was hot and spicy.

The people are angry and frustrated is a sentence because it has a verb (*are*).

The angry and frustrated people is a noun phrase. It does not have a verb.

Noun phrases with adjectives are useful because they pack more information into the sentence. For example

The angry, frustrated people marched noisily to the town hall.

The sentence *The people are angry and frustrated.* cannot be developed in this way.

4 Add an adjective *before* each of the following two nouns.

The aeroplane

The yacht

You should have two short noun phrases. Place the verb *sped* after each of your two noun phrases and complete two descriptive sentences.

> So far in this unit, you have seen how a basic noun phrase can be built up with adjectives. A single noun like *proposals* can be made to provide more detail in a phrase: *these absurd proposals.* Prepositions too can increase the detail in noun phrases. Remember that prepositions are words like *in*, *with*, *on* and *under* that are used before nouns.
>
> *the absurd proposals in the mayor's pocket*
>
> is a very long noun phrase made up of two short ones.

5   a Which noun phrase in the original passage is like this?

   b What is the preposition that links the noun phrases together?

A pair of adjectives before a noun can be joined with *and*. Only do this in your own writing if you are sure of the effect you want to create. It is more usual to leave out the *and* in favour of a comma. The two different ways are shown below.

This green and pleasant land

This green, pleasant land

How did I do?

I can include adjectives in noun phrases.   □

12: Creating mood

In this unit you will learn
▶ to consider the creation of mood

Get started

In the following extract, a twelve-year-old boy describes sitting in a waiting room.

> There was a shelf of dusty books that were always in the same order. Above them was a lonely spider plant that drooped down sadly. On a table in the middle of the room were some crumpled, glossy magazines. Their covers showed shiny faces beaming out fantastic smiles.

This is an extremely *visual* description. The writer creates mood by relating what he sees. The first thing the writer describes is the books on the shelf.

Practice

1 a What adjective does the writer use to describe the books?

   b What else does he notice about the books?

   c What does the writer seem to be suggesting about these books?

Remember that a noun phrase is a word or a group of words that describe a central noun.

a shelf of dusty books is a noun phrase.

2 a Write down the two noun phrases used by the writer to describe *a plant* and *some magazines.* Both noun phrases are four words in length.

   b Select one word from each noun phrase that adds to the gloomy mood the writer wants to create.

The second sentence uses personification. **Personification** is a form of metaphor that gives character and life to things that are not human. To describe a plant as *lonely,* for example, is not logical, as a plant cannot have feelings. This is to miss the point of personification, though. By describing the plant in this way, the writer conveys a sense of the mood in the waiting room.

3 At the end of the second sentence, the writer continues the use of personification. What adverb does he use to personify the plant at the end of the sentence?

The adverb at the end of the second sentence modifies a verb that is also used to create a rather mournful mood.

4 What is the verb that is modified at the end of the second sentence?

One of the most effective techniques of description open to a writer is the use of contrast. This is not surprising, really, when you think of some examples from everyday life. Stars, for instance, are in the sky the whole time. It is only when it's dark that you see them because they contrast with the blackness of the night.

In the passage about the waiting room, the writer wants to create a mood that is in tune with his own gloomy feelings as he waits for the dentist. He highlights and emphasises this mood with the contrasts introduced at the end.

5 a Which adjectives are used in the final sentence to emphasise the faces and the smiles on the magazines' covers?

    b Remember the continuous participle. It is created by adding *ing* to the infinitive form of a verb. Which participle suggests the way the faces and smiles shine out from the magazines?

    c How does the real world of the waiting room contrast with the make-believe world of the magazines?

 Use foregrounded prepositional phrases to create variety in your own writing.

It is important to vary word order in sentences. If sentences are not varied, then writing, even in short extracts like this, can become repetitive. One of the easiest and most effective ways of varying sentence structure is by foregrounding prepositional phrases. In the third sentence the writer of the extract foregrounds the phrase *On a table*.

On a table in the middle of the room were some crumpled, glossy magazines.

This could have been written

Some crumpled, glossy magazines were on a table in the middle of the room.

The writer also foregrounds a prepositional phrase at the start of the second sentence.

6 Rearrange the sentence using the example above as your guide.

Now reread the whole passage with the reorganised sentences. Notice how repetitive it seems.

How did I do?

I know how to consider the creation of mood. ✔ ☐

1 Identify the five nouns in the following list.

mask angrily because much occasion surprise be key planet pushed

2 Look at the following nouns and noun phrases. Find

a   five nouns

b   three adjectives

c   three determiners

pear

spiralling costs

some students

my eager friends

the lonely plant

3 The phrases that follow each consist of two noun phrases joined with a preposition. Identify

a   six noun phrases

b   three prepositions

a web in the dark corner

my uncle with some relations

that excellent café at the crossroads

4 a   Each of the verbs in these three sentences is followed by an adverbial phrase. Identify the three verbs used in these sentences.

The seed waited under the winter snow.

Jake disappeared in a desperate panic.

I work during daylight.

b   Write down the three prepositions used directly after each verb.

c   Foreground the adverbial phrase in each of the three sentences. Remember to separate each phrase from the rest of its sentence with a comma.

5 What is the name of the descriptive technique used in the following sentence?

His skin was as cracked as a dry leaf.

6 In each of the following sentences a main verb in its infinitive form is modified by the modal verb that comes before it. Write down the

a   five modal verbs

b   five main verbs

People should be more thoughtful.

The big bad wolf might get you.

The new speed humps may calm the traffic.

She can speak German.

We could put it here.

7 a The following passage is held together with noun references to the subject (or topic) noun, *fruit flies*. Make a reference chain that includes all the nouns, pronouns and noun phrases used in the extract to refer to fruit flies.

> Fruit flies are back. These infuriating creatures cover my strawberries every summer. They don't actually destroy anything. They don't really seem to **do** anything. They are, however, in my opinion, insect vermin.

    b Which pronoun is used three times to refer back to the fruit flies?

    c Look again at the two noun phrases in your reference chain. What do they tell you about the writer's attitude towards fruit flies?

8 The following two sentences have been written in the simple present tense.

He swims for us.

They break their promises.

Write them out in the

    a present perfect tense

    b past perfect tense

    c present continuous tense

    d past continuous tense

9 Why is the verb *do* sometimes placed before a verb in its infinitive form?

10 Look at these pairs of six clauses. Join each pair with a connective to make three complex sentences.

Mark went straight home	*he had left our house.*
Bring something to eat	*you want to come with us.*
They were still in the park	*the downpour started.*

14: Formal and informal

In this unit you will learn
▶ to adapt style to audience and purpose

Get started

There is no right or wrong writing style. There are simply many styles to choose from. Some of them will be right on one occasion. Others will be right on different occasions. Learning when to use the range of available styles is an important part of becoming a better writer.

Style refers to the way you choose to write. Read this extract from an e-mail circular.

> Hi guys! Sorry not to have been in touch for so long. I'm in Australia now (whooeee!) and here's my new address.

The writer uses a **relaxed style**, which is signalled at the opening of her e-mail.

Practice

1
  a Which two words does the writer use at the start of her e-mail to create informality?

  b What punctuation mark does she use twice to suggest energy and fun?

  c Which onomatopoeic (sound related) word does she use to show her excitement?

Remember that sometimes an adjective can follow a verb to describe a subject. For example

I am happy.

Donna is pleased.

In very informal writing, the initial subject and the verb can be missed out as follows.

Happy you could make it!

Pleased that you could come!

2 Write out the sentence from the e-mail in which the writer uses this informal technique.

Contraction of words is also a sign of informality. This happens when writers join two words with an apostrophe and 'lose' letters to imitate speech. For example

will not   becomes   *won't*

he will   becomes   *he'll*

3   a Write down the two contracted forms in the e-mail.

   b What would be the formal way of writing out these words?

The writer of the e-mail used exactly the right sort of style for her purpose. She wanted to communicate with her friends in a way that was clear, purposeful, fun and relaxed. And this is exactly what she did. As it happens, however, the same author writes instructions for flat pack manuals. The following extract is from one of her leaflets.

> Press down firmly with both hands. Next, push the rockers into place. The chair is now ready to use.

These are instructions. The writing contains features of an **instructional style** in just the same way as the informal e-mail had *its* own special features.

A feature of instructions is that they need to be laid out clearly according to what happens when. This means that adverbs describing *when* things happen are common. These include words like

soon   *firstly*   *now*   *next*   *then*   *finally*

4   Which two adverbs from this list can you find in the flat pack text?

Both the e-mail message *and* the instructions do their own jobs. One gives information in a friendly way and one gives instructions clearly. Neither extract is better than the other and both use their own techniques. Make sure that in your own writing you adapt your style to purpose in just the same way.

Most sentences have a subject and a verb. You have already seen how this rule can be broken in certain types of informal writing. However, writing to instruct also breaks this rule. Subjects are often missed out in order to give a direct instruction. For example

grind the pepper   not   *you* grind the pepper

whisk the eggs   not   *you* whisk the eggs

screw down the lid   not   *you* screw down the lid

5   Write down the two sentences in the extract that use this technique.

How did I do?

I can adapt style to audience and purpose.   ✔ ☐

15: Explanations

In this unit you will learn
  ▶ to analyse writing that explains

Get started

In the following extract, a Year 10 student, Rebecca Hanley, explains why she opted for History at the end of Year 9.

> I've always liked history, even in Juniors where you do the Saxons and Romans. I love all the action. There's always something going on. I like studying how people behaved in different centuries. They were so different to us. People had to put up with things that we can't imagine today. Epidemics, witch hunts, famines – it seems impossible from our comfortable position looking back.

Practice

1 a When does the writer say she became interested in history?

  b Which periods of history was she particularly interested in when she was younger?

  c Name three things the writer says that people had to put up with in the past.

Look again at the following two sentences.

I love all the action.

They were so different to us.

The verbs are in different tenses.

2 a Which verbs are used in each sentence?

  b Write down the verb tense used in each of the two sentences.

  c Explain why the writer changes verb tense.

Rebecca goes on to explain why she thinks so few girls at her school do History.

> I think the first reason that girls don't opt for History at our school is because there are no women teachers. Some of my friends would definitely have done it if there had been. The second reason is more important, though. It is because history itself is full of men. Think about it. History is full of male superheroes!

ⓘ Rebecca gives the word *History* a capital *H* when she is writing about it as a school subject. At these times she uses it as a proper noun. At other times, she uses the word (with a small *h*) as a common noun simply to refer to the past.

3   a   What two reasons does the writer give for girls not doing History at her school?

     b   What matching pair of three-word noun phrases does the writer use to highlight the fact that she is providing reasons in a logical order?

     c   Who does the writer say would have done History if there had been women teachers?

     d   Which adverb indicates she is certain that her statement about her friends is true?

A small number of adverbs can be used to show that a statement already made is about to be modified. One of these adverbs is *however.* Adverbs like *however* are used like this.

Apples contain Vitamin C. Blackcurrants contain more, however.

The statement about apples is modified in the light of the evidence about blackcurrants. Notice how the adverb is sectioned off with a comma.

4   Rebecca uses an adverb in a similar way to this in the extract. Write out the sentence in which an adverb is used in a similar way to *however.*

Imperative sentences are those that use an infinitive form of a verb and omit a subject. For example

Print out a copy.

Tell me again.

Show me the reason.

They are used in this sort of writing to show a kind of friendly directness. Rebecca knows her idea is controversial and she wants the reader to consider it.

5   Write out her imperative sentence.

Rebecca increases the dramatic impact of her idea at the end of her passage.

6   How does she highlight her unusual idea in the closing sentence?

How did I do?

I know how to analyse writing that explains.   ✔ ☐

16: Features of argument

Get started

Some people argue that schools should replace the current three-term year with one of five shorter terms. The following extract is from an article that takes this view.

> Many schools around the country are becoming interested in setting up a five-term year. At present, a majority still run the outdated three-term system. Some progressive schools, however, are already making the change.

The verb *become* does not, like many verbs, describe an action. It is similar to verbs such as *be, appear* and *seem*, which are all called verbs of *state*. **Verbs of state** can be used with adjectives, like this.

*He is **becoming** angry.*

*She **appears** friendly.*

*They all **seem** happy.*

The verb *become* can be very useful in its present continuous form (*is becoming/are becoming*). This is because it creates the sense of something growing.

Compare   *He is angry.*   with   *He is becoming angry.*

The second sentence suggests that the anger is growing in a gradual way.

Practice

1 In the passage above, the writer uses *becoming* in a continuous form. What does she suggest is growing?

Determiners go before nouns to tell us more about them. In the following phrases, the pattern of words is determiner + noun.

His phone

The river

Many people

A tooth

Some grapes

In arguments, determiners can be used cleverly to suggest that lots of people are on your side.

2 Write down the determiner + noun combination at the beginning of the passage that indicates that lots of people are on the writer's side.

Even the choice of grammatical words like determiners can be important in argument.

Every panda in the world is a noun phrase. It is made up of two smaller noun phrases (*every panda* and *the world*) that are linked by the preposition *in.* Noun phrases like this come before or after a verb as follows.

Every panda in the world *eats bamboo.* (before the verb *eats*)

We must protect **every panda in the world**. (after the verb *protect*)

3 a In the passage about school term there is an example of a five-word noun phrase formed in just the same way as the panda noun phrase. Write down the five-word noun phrase that is formed in this way.

b This noun phrase is used by the writer to suggest people agree with her. How do the last three words of the noun phrase show this?

Sometimes adjectives can be placed between determiners and nouns in noun phrases to make the pattern determiner + adjective + noun. The following noun phrases follow this pattern.

Every **sensible** *panda*

All **broken** *glass*

The **thoughtful** *present*

4 a In the last sentence of the extract there is a three-word noun phrase that follows the same pattern as the examples above. Write down the three-word noun phrase.

b What is suggested by the adjective in this noun phrase?

The outdated three-term system is a noun phrase based on the noun *system.*

5 a What adjectives are used in this noun phrase?

b What does the noun phrase suggest the writer would like to happen to the three-term year?

Revision booster

The adverb *already* is often used by writers as follows.
Gene-centred robotics is tomorrow's technology. We **already** *use it.*

6 What does the writer of the extract suggest with her use of *already*?

How did I do?

I can assess features of argument. ☐

17: Punctuating sentences

In this unit you will learn
- ▶ to punctuate at boundaries

Get started

Many people, at one time or another, have produced a sentence that looks like this.

The soldier sharpened his knife, he walked down the trench, he checked everyone's equipment, a rat bit his ankle.

The sentence needs proper punctuation. It would lose marks in any test.

The first step towards proper sentence punctuation is to be able to identify clauses. Clauses contain a verb. The verb may consist of one or more words. For example

sharpen

has sharpened

will be sharpening

One you've found the verb, you need to find the subject of the clause. In other words, the person or thing that performs the action of the verb.

Practice

1 a Who or what performs the action of the verb *sharpen* in the first clause of the sentence above?

   b Who or what performs the action of the verb *bit* in the last clause?

Like the verb, the subject may consist of one or more words.

2 Write down each different subject of the verb *sharpen* in the following clauses.

The scout sharpened

She sharpened

The merry barber with the wide grin sharpened

Imagine you've identified the subject and the verb of a clause. You then need to see if there is anything following the verb that relates to either it or the subject. Often there will be another noun that forms what's called the *object* of the verb.

*The barber sharpened **his razor**.*

Sometimes a preposition is followed by a noun phrase to create a prepositional phrase.

*The soldier walked **up the hill**.*

3　a　What is the object of the verb *sharpen* in the first clause of the sentence at the beginning of this unit?

　　b　What is the object of *checked* in the third clause?

　　c　What is the object of *bit* in the final clause?

　　d　What is the prepositional phrase following *walked* in the second clause?

The sentence about the soldier contains four separate clauses.

4　How does the writer separate the clauses from one another?

Clauses can be separated from one another with full stops. This would create a properly punctuated text like this.

> The soldier sharpened his knife. He walked down the trench. He checked everyone's equipment. A rat bit his ankle.

This text is now *correct* but it does not flow very well. It uses single-verb clauses as sentences and before long this makes a text boring.

Instead of separating the clauses, you can join them with connectives. Connectives join a pair of clauses like this.

*The barber sharpened his razor **as** he talked to his friend.*

Alternatively, your connective can go at the start of the sentence with the second clause.

***As** he talked to his friend, the barber sharpened his razor.*

Notice that the second (or **subordinate**) clause is now sectioned off with a comma.

You can also change *talk* into its continuous participle and join the clauses that way.

***Talking to his friend**, the barber sharpened his razor.*

5　Use each of these three techniques to join the first two clauses in the soldier text.

 In well-punctuated writing, clauses are either clearly separated or clearly joined.

How did I do?

I know how to punctuate at boundaries.　□

18: Literary verse

In this unit you will learn
▶ to evaluate poetry in the literary tradition

Get started

Read the following poem called *The Eagle.* It was written by a famous poet named Tennyson.

He clasps the crag with crooked hands
Close to the sun in lonely lands,
Ring'd with the azure world, he stands.

The wrinkled sea beneath him crawls;
He watches from his mountain walls,
And like a thunderbolt he falls.

Practice

On line 5, the reader discovers that the eagle is perched high on a mountain. Tennyson, however, has already hinted at this earlier on in the poem.

1   a Which single word in line 1 suggests the eagle is in a rocky place?

b Which four-word phrase in line 2 suggests the eagle is high up?

Adjectives and verbs can often be used in unusual ways to create dramatic effects.

2   a Which adjective is used to describe the sea?

b What verb is used to describe the way the sea is moving?

The sea is being described as the eagle might see it.

3   What does the description in line 4 suggest about the distance between the eagle and the sea?

Alliteration is a word used to describe the poetic technique of placing lots of similar sounds near to one another. Look at this example.

In the soft,
Too silken silence.

The poet uses alliteration on the letter *s* to help create a sugary impression of peace and calm that is perhaps a little *too* smooth and silent. In *The Eagle*, Tennyson uses alliteration on the 'hard c' (the *c* as in car).

4   a   Write down five words in the poem that contain the hard c.

      b   Which word contains the sound twice?

      c   Why might the poet have wanted to emphasise this hard sound?

Remember that a simile is the direct comparison of one thing and another, often introduced with the word *like*.

The tiger's claws were like spears.

In this simile the tiger's claws are compared to spears. It is never enough just to identify such comparisons, though. You need, as a reader, to explain the effect.

5   a   What is the effect of comparing claws to spears?

      b   What does the eagle *fall like* in the poem?

      c   What is suggested about the eagle by this simile?

Similes are direct comparisons. Metaphors make comparisons in a less direct way. Metaphors *suggest* links and connections. For example

*The wall of stones **refused** to budge.*

Stones, of course, cannot *refuse* to do anything. The writer *imagines* them as human to create a comparison between the stone wall and a person refusing to budge.

In the poem, the eagle is made to seem more like us (humans) in a word used instead of *claws*.

6   Which word does the poet use to make the eagle seem more human?

Revision booster

The action of the first five lines in the poem is quite different from that of the last line.

7   a   What atmosphere is created in the first five lines of the poem?

      b   Which two words in line 5 sum up the eagle's actions until that point?

      c   The last line seems to explain the eagle's earlier actions. What do you think the eagle might be doing in the last line?

How did I do?

I know how to evaluate poetry in the literary tradition.

19: Using adverbs

In this unit you will learn
▶ to use adverbs and adverbial phrases

Get started

Remember that adverbs usually describe verbs. They often tell a reader how or in what way some action was carried out. For example

*The giant slept **soundly**.*   (in a sound way)

*The archaeologist worked **hard**.*   (in a hard way)

Practice

1 Finish off the following short sentences with suitable adverbs.

The work progressed   (in a slow way)

Music was played   (in a loud way)

Adverbs can also tell a reader *when* an action occurs. Common adverbs of time are

next   now   then   tomorrow   yesterday   again   immediately   soon presently   later

2 Pick out five adverbs of time from the following passage.

> I went diving yesterday. Now I know what all the fuss is about. I'm going again soon and I can't wait until then.

Adverbs can provide information about *where* something takes place. Common adverbs of place are

outside   here   there   underneath   in   over   through   out

3 Complete the following with a single adverb of place from the list above.

The house is warm. Come ...

The door's open. Go ...

There's a cloth on the table. You won't see the mark unless you look ...

Adverbs of degree often describe adjectives and other adverbs. They give the reader details about *how much* something is done. For example

really   incredibly   rather   very   too   extremely   just   quite   hardly   totally

4 Write down the six adverbs of degree in the following passage.

> I'm totally furious with Jocasta. She's been rather mean to me and incredibly nasty to Lucinda. I'm afraid it's just too bad. I'm going to get very cross if it goes on.

The job of adverbs is very often done not by single words but by phrases. For example

The planes will land **at the same time**.

Go **to the Science Block**.

She walked out **in a fury**.

Notice that these adverbial phrases can often be replaced by a single adverb that means almost the same thing. For example

The planes will land **simultaneously**.

Go **there**.

She walked out **furiously**.

5 Replace the following adverbial phrases with a single adverb.

Come **to me**.

The crowd disappeared **in an instant**.

Yours is **after this one**.

Adverbs and adverbial phrases can often be included in sentences in various places. For example

Suddenly, she left.   She suddenly left.   She left suddenly.

Notice that the adverb is usually followed by a comma if it goes at the start of a sentence.

6 Take the adverb *constantly* and add it to the following sentence in as many different positions as you can. You should be able to include the adverb in four different positions.

He thought about it.

 Adverbs can often be moved to different positions within sentences without changing their meaning. Altering the position of adverbs is therefore a good way to create variety.

How did I do?

I can use adverbs and adverbial phrases.

20: Persuasive techniques

In this unit you will learn
- to understand persuasive techniques

Get started

This extract is from a letter recently sent out by a primary school. It persuades parents to get involved in the school fair.

> Are you fit? Do you have a sense of humour? Can you give up a couple of hours of your time for a very worthy cause next Saturday afternoon? If you can, you could be just the person we are looking for. We need enthusiastic and energetic people like you to help with our school fair.

Remember that the personal pronouns are

I/me   you   he/him   she/her   it   we/us   they/them

Practice

1 a Which personal pronoun is used throughout the passage to address the reader?

  b Why do you think persuasive writing often refers to the reader in this way?

Rhetorical questions are another common feature of persuasive writing. These are questions that do not need a reply. The reader is expected to ask the questions of him- or herself. In the case of this letter, the answers can only be either *yes* or *no*.

2 a How many rhetorical questions are asked in this extract?

  b How would most people wish to answer the opening two questions?

  c What effect does the writer hope this will have on the answer to the final question?

Now look again at the final rhetorical question. It contains three phrases that are important for the persuasive impact of the letter. The phrases are

a couple of hours

your time

a very worthy cause

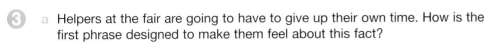

3   a   Helpers at the fair are going to have to give up their own time. How is the first phrase designed to make them feel about this fact?

b   What does the second phrase show about the writer's attitude to the time being given?

c   In what way is the third phrase persuasive?

<table>
<tr><td>Persuasive writing often flatters its readers.</td></tr>
</table>

You have already seen how the first two rhetorical questions are designed to lead readers into answers that are flattering. This light-hearted flattery continues at the end of the letter when the writer assumes that the reader is a certain type of person.

4   Which two adjectives used in the final sentence make an assumption that flatters the reader?

Persuasive writing often flatters its readers. In addition, it sometimes emphasises the neediness of the writer. One way of doing this, of course, is to ask direct questions of the reader. Another is through the verbs used to express what is wanted.

5   a   Which four-word phrase used in the fourth sentence suggests the writer is searching?

b   Write down the pronoun and verb used at the start of the final sentence.

c   What is the final verb used in the extract?

Look at the words and phrases you have extracted from the text for this task. See how they communicate a very clear message indeed.

Revision booster

Determiners are words like

my   his   the   their   a

They are used before nouns and noun phrases, like this

a school fair

the school fair

any school fair

6   a   What determiner is used for the *school fair* in the extract?

b   What does the determiner suggest about the writer's attitude towards the fair?

How did I do?

I understand persuasive techniques.   ☐

21: Range of perspectives

In this unit you will learn
  ▶ to convey a range of perspectives

Get started

It is important that, where necessary, you learn how to convey a range of perspectives or points of view. People have different angles on any interesting question. As a writer you need to be able to express them, as well as explaining your own.

A council in Dorset recently asked its residents for their opinions on plans to build a skateboarding area within existing parkland. This is part of one of the many responses they received.

> I feel strongly that many people would benefit from having this new skateboard park. At present, teenagers have nowhere to go after school. They are bored and can get involved in crimes such as vandalism and shoplifting. If there was a new area in the park, they would have somewhere of their own. Now consider the toddlers who won't even use the park. They will have the existing play area all to themselves. They won't have to dodge out of the way of older kids who don't have anywhere else to go. Their mums and dads would benefit as well. Some people think that a skateboard park might cause problems. I believe it would solve them.

Practice

1. The writer accounts for many viewpoints. Locate them by answering these questions. Your answers should consist of nouns and noun phrases (such as *the man* or *children* or *boys and girls*) taken from the text.

   a Who would benefit from having the new skateboard park?

   b Who has nowhere to go after school?

   c Who won't even use the park?

   d Who would benefit as well?

   e Who thinks that the skateboard park might cause problems?

   f Who believes it would solve them?

   g How many different viewpoints are conveyed in this text?

2. a According to the writer, how do teenagers in the area currently feel?

   b How do many teenagers seem to respond to these feelings at present?

   c How would the skateboard park improve toddlers' play time?

   d How would toddlers' parents benefit from the skateboard park?

Writers can convey their own viewpoints and those of others by using a noun or a noun phrase before verbs that express belief, such as

I believe

they consider

teenagers feel

The impression that these beliefs are held strongly can be communicated by the use of adverbs and adverbial phrases that express *how much* or *in what way* the beliefs are held.

*I **firmly** believe*

*teenagers feel **passionately***

*they consider **in a rational way***

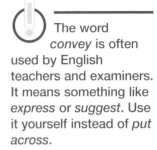

The word *convey* is often used by English teachers and examiners. It means something like *express* or *suggest*. Use it yourself instead of *put across*.

3   a   Which phrase does the writer use to express her own beliefs at the start of the text?

b   Which verb is used to express the ideas of *some people* who disagree with her?

c   Which verb is used to sum up her feelings at the end?

The writer uses a further verb of belief in the middle of the passage. She writes

Now consider the toddlers who won't even use the park.

She is not expressing or conveying a viewpoint here. She is acknowledging that another important point of view exists.

4   a   Which people exactly is the writer asking to *consider the toddlers*?

b   Why is the viewpoint of these people such an important one?

Revision booster

In the middle of the passage the writer uses the phrase *somewhere of their own* to describe the way teenagers would feel about a new skateboard park.

There are two phrases in the text used to contrast with this vision of the future. They describe where teenagers have to go at present.

5   Find and write down these two phrases.

How did I do?

I can convey a range of perspectives.

✔

22: Structuring sentences

In this unit you will learn
- ▶ to structure sentences

Get started

One of the most basic sentence structures consists of a subject, a verb and an adverb.

The **subject** of a sentence is *what* the sentence is about. You can identify the subject by asking *who* or *what* did the verb. For example

He ate spinach.	*Who* ate spinach?	*He* did	So *He* is the subject
The mug broke.	*What* broke?	*The mug* broke	So *The mug* is the subject

Practice

1 Write down the subjects of the following three sentences.

I took it to her.

Beach fashions are cool.

The enormous crocodile was hungry.

Notice that the subject of a sentence can be a single noun or a noun phrase. A noun phrase is an expression used for groups of words used as single nouns. For example

Suns   Our sun   The warm sun   The bright warm sun
The bright sun in the blue sky

None of these noun phrases contains a verb. If they did they would not be noun phrases. All of the above can be used as the subject of a sentence.

Suns give light.

Our sun is quite small.

The bright sun in the blue sky shone down warmly.

If you ask the following questions you will find the subjects of each of these three sentences.

What gives light?

What is quite small?

What shone down warmly?

The **verb** in a sentence is the *action* word or the word that describes the *state* of something. For example

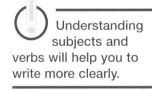

Understanding subjects and verbs will help you to write more clearly.

Harry **is walking** in the field.	*is walking* describes Harry's *actions*
Angelina **danced**.	*danced* describes Angelina's *actions*
They **seem** unhappy.	*seem* describes the *state* of being unhappy
She **appears** cold.	*appears* describes the *state* of being cold

Notice that, as with the subject of a sentence, a verb can contain more than one word.

2 Identify the verbs in the following sentences.

The water is running down the hill.

She has seemed unwell for a long time.

The wind blows wildly.

Sentences often contain **adverbs** or **adverbial phrases** (sometimes called **adverbials**) that add detail to the verb. We can choose either a single adverb or a group of words.

Harry is walking **in the field**.	gives detail about *where* the action occurs
The wind blows **wildly**.	gives detail about *how* the action occurs
We leave **in a moment**.	gives detail about *when* the action occurs

3 Identify the adverbs and adverbial phrases in the following sentences.

He waited at the corner.

Angelina danced all night long.

She murmured quietly.

Revision booster

The subject, the verb and the adverb can all be developed within this sentence structure. For example

He waited at the corner can become

The old man (expanded noun phrase) *is waiting* (longer verb) *in the lamplight at the corner* (expanded adverbial phrase).

4 Develop the following sentence in the same way.

She murmured quietly.

How did I do?

I know how to structure sentences.

23: What if?

In this unit you will learn
- to express possibility

Get started

Some people believe that a number of UFOs containing alien life forms crashed into the American desert in the 1950s. In this extract from *ExtraTerrestrial,* one such person expresses his hope that aliens are being held by the army and could be released for interview one day.

> It seems likely that aliens crashed into New Mexico on June 12th 1957. Traces of the accident were removed immediately. If the aliens are still alive then they are probably being held at a military installation beneath the desert. An interview with one of these aliens would be a dream for most of us. It is a dream that might be about to come true.

Likelihood can be expressed in formal language using the following construction.

It + is/appears/seems + adjective + that

The adjective you place in the structure above will be one of a limited number expressing possibility. For example

possible/impossible   likely/unlikely   certain/not certain   probable/improbable

The sentences that emerge will be similar to these.

It is unlikely that *climate change can be reversed.*

It appears probable that *the road will be built.*

Practice

① Write down the sentence in the aliens extract above that follows this pattern.

② Now *remove* the first four words of the sentence you just wrote down.

  a What is the effect of removing these four words?

  b Why do you think the writer chose to include them in his text?

> Words often take on different forms (for example, *possible* and *possibly*) to play different parts in sentences.

Look again at the list of adjectives above. Most of them can be changed into adverbs that also express likelihood and chance. For example, *possible* and *certain* (adjectives) can function as *possibly* and *certainly* (adverbs).

③ Which *one* adjective from the list above has been modified in the text to make an adverb?

Sentences that use *if* and *then* are common in writing that expresses possibility. The *if* statement, for example

If you like hot curry

If the prisoners are innocent

normally expresses the possibility which, if it's proved true, will create the situation expressed in the second part of the sentence.

If you like hot curry, then you should try vindaloo.

If the prisoners are innocent, then release them straightaway.

4 Find the *if ... then* sentence in the aliens extract.

   a What possibility is expressed by the *if* statement?

   b What situation is suggested by the *then* statement?

Modal verbs are normally used before the infinitive form of main verbs. Modal verbs include the following.

might   could   can   would   should   may

They modify the meaning of main verbs as follows.

She **might** go home.

She **can** go home.

As you can see, modals affect the same main verb in different ways.

5 a Which two modal verbs (from the list above) are used in the passage?

   b Which infinitive form of a main verb do they both modify?

The modal in the last sentence expresses possibility since the writer is unsure of future events.

6 a What does the modal in the penultimate (second to last) sentence express?

   b Why does the writer feel like this?

How did I do?

I know how to express possibility. ✔ ☐

24: Spelling homophones

In this unit you will learn
> to spell common homophones

Get started

Homophones are words that *sound* the same as each other but which are spelled differently. For example

cereal   spelled in this way is something you eat   *but*

serial   spelled like this is a story told in separate parts

hair   spelled in this way is something you might comb   *but*

hare   spelled like this is an animal quite similar to a rabbit

Practice

1   Write down homophones for the following six words.

flour   waist   through   knight   right   piece

Now look at these words.

everywhere   here   somewhere   nowhere   where   there   anywhere

2   a What concept do all these words refer to?

   b Which four letters appear at the ends of all these words?

Taken together, these two facts provide a useful spelling rule:

The common *place* words all end with *here*. Other words with a similar sound are spelled differently, and have different meanings.

here refers to a place	*hear* is what you do with your ears	
where refers to a place	*wear* is what you do with clothes	*we're* is *we are*
there refers to a place	*their* is a determiner like *my* and *your*	*they're* is *they are*

The apostrophes should be easy to remember: if your meaning is *they are* or *we are* (or *it is*, *you are*, *there is*) then the spelling of that word is *they're* or *we're* (or *it's*, *you're*, *there's*).

Remember from previous units that determiners are words like *their*, *his*, *your* and *my*. They go before nouns like this.

their problem   **my** coat   **his** future   **her** suggestion

So something that *belongs to them* uses the determiner *their*.

③ Use the rules in this unit to correct the following mistakes.

Their driving over now.	*There not doing it properly.*
Hear comes the bus.	*Did he where a tie?*
He doesn't know wear it is.	*Sit over their.*
They like they're new house.	*Theirs a problem.*
I can't here you very well.	*The problem is there's.*

> The homophones covered in this unit are often misspelled in tests. Make sure you know them well, so that you can use them even when you are under pressure.

It is very common for *its* and *it's* to be confused. Remember these rules.

The full spelling of *it's* is *it is*; *it's* uses an apostrophe to show that a letter has been removed (in this case *i*). It works in the same way as other words that have been shortened.

it is	becomes	*it's*
there is	becomes	*there's*
here is	becomes	*here's*

If you can replace *it's* in a sentence with *it is*, then you know you have used it correctly.

Its without an apostrophe is a determiner that defines a noun, just like *their*.

For example, *You shouldn't judge a book by **its** cover*.

④ Are the following uses of *its/it's* correct or incorrect?

Its a beautiful day today.

The team has lost it's best player.

I think that its too far to walk.

The snake shed it's skin.

How did I do?

I can spell common homophones.

25: Shakespeare

In this unit you will learn

▶ to examine a speech from Shakespeare

Get started

The passage that follows is from *Othello,* one of Shakespeare's tragedies. Othello is a great general in the Venetian army. He fears that his wife, Desdemona, is being unfaithful to him. She can't find a present he once gave her, a handkerchief, and he sees this as a bad omen.

Read what Othello says to Desdemona about the missing handkerchief.

... that handkerchief
Did an Egyptian to my mother give,
She was a charmer, and could almost read   [charmer – clairvoyant]
The thoughts of people; she told her, while she kept it
'Twould make her amiable, and subdue my father   [amiable – desirable]
Entirely to her love: but if she lost it,
Or made a gift of it, my father's eye
Should hold her loathly, and his spirits should hunt
After new fancies: she dying, gave it me,
And bid me, when my fate would have me wive,
To give it her; I did so, and take heed on't,
Make it a darling, like your precious eye,
To lose, or give't away, were such perdition   [perdition – hell]
As nothing else could match.

Practice

1 a Who gave the handkerchief to Othello's mother?

   b When exactly did Othello's mother give him the handkerchief?

   c What did Othello's mother tell him to do with the handkerchief?

Othello believes the handkerchief has magic powers.

2 a What does Othello say the clairvoyant could 'almost' do?

   b How would the handkerchief make Othello's mother appear to her husband?

   c If she lost the handkerchief, what would her husband's 'spirits' hunt after?

Othello is worried about the effects of losing this handkerchief.

3 What does he ask Desdemona to 'make' the handkerchief?

Look at the use of the word *eye* in this passage. We still have the expression *wandering* or *roving eye* to describe the attitude of someone who cannot remain faithful to a single partner.

4
a Whose eye is referred to first in this passage?

b How will this eye 'hold' Othello's mother if the handkerchief is lost?

c Othello wants to believe that Desdemona does not have a wandering eye. What adjective does he use to describe her eye (her faithfulness)?

d Where does Othello believe they will all go if Desdemona's faithfulness (and the handkerchief) is lost?

As it happens, Desdemona has not been unfaithful at all. One of Othello's fellow soldiers, Iago, is making trouble between the two of them because he is a horribly envious man. Othello doesn't really have any good reason to suspect his wife.

5 In a sentence or two, summarise the impression you gain of Othello from his speech. You should write about both his attitude towards the handkerchief and his reaction to its apparent loss.

At the end of the play, Othello is wrongly convinced that Desdemona has been unfaithful and he murders her.

Othello's speech gives us some interesting examples of the way English has changed since Shakespeare's time.

6 Look at the unusual sentence structure used in the first two lines. Write these lines out in modern English using a structure we would be more familiar with. Change as few words as possible.

7 Othello uses the noun *charmer* to mean a clairvoyant. How is the word used nowadays?

8 Today the verb *wive* has almost fallen out of use. What action does Othello describe when he uses this verb?

9 Othello uses an adverb *loathly* that has also nearly fallen out of use. What related verb do we still have that suggests the action of strong hatred?

10 Othello uses the contractions *'Twould* and *on't*. We still use contractions in English, but not these ones. Write these contractions out as unshortened phrases.

How did I do?

I can examine a speech from Shakespeare.

1 Each of the following sentences finishes with an adverbial phrase. Phrases like these can often be foregrounded (moved to the start of the sentence) in order to provide clarity and contrast.

Rewrite all these sentences with foregrounded adverbial phrases, using a comma in the appropriate place each time.

There are many life forms under the earth.

She vanished into the dark night.

The beach changes completely around eight o'clock.

2 The following noun phrases are made up of a determiner added to a noun. Expand these phrases by placing appropriate adjectives between the determiner and the noun that follows in each case.

This crowd

Many windows

The waterfall

3 Develop these clauses by placing an adjective *after* the verb provided.

The building appears

These forests are

That old metal has gone

4 The *subject* of a sentence is identified by asking *who* or *what* did the action of the verb. The subject can consist of a pronoun, a noun or a noun phrase made up of a number of words.

Identify the subjects of the following sentences.

The small boy is sharpening his pencil.

She smiled sweetly.

Oranges are delicious at the moment.

The Power Rangers costume will be arriving tomorrow.

5 Remember that verbs, too, can be made up of one word or more than one word. Write down the verbs used in each sentence from the question above.

6 The following poorly punctuated passage contains four subjects and four verbs. On this occasion, each of the verbs consists of a single word. The subjects in this passage are made up of either a noun, a pronoun or a noun phrase.

> Martha walked through the mall she went into her favourite café all her friends smiled at her she chatted to them.

Write down each subject and verb combination. The first one is done for you.

Martha walked

7 Each verb is followed by a qualifying phrase. The first two are prepositional phrases and the second two adverbial phrases. Write them out and identify them.

8 Now you can punctuate the four sentences correctly. Write them out with full stops and capital letters in the right places.

9 Place the adverb *instantly* into the following sentence in as many different places as makes sense. Remember to use a comma if necessary.

Euan changed his mind.

10 *Some* of these sentences contain common mistakes in the use of apostrophes or spelling. Correct the individual words that contain errors.

The students took their text books to the laboratory.

He doesn't know whether its raining outside.

Their always complaining about things.

The horse reared up angrily on it's hind legs.

I don't think she realises your coming to the party.

I felt as if I was up their in the sky.

Answers

1 Prepositions

1 *monkey, sadness, apple, story, invitation*
2 *a, the, every, that, some, their*
3 a *in, on, with, over, under, at*
  b *a, every, this, some*
4 *The Queen never seems to be at home. A dangerous troll is said to live over this mountain. The train from Leeds is on time. This rare beetle was unfortunately squashed under some books. I think more about you with every minute.*
5 *At most, we have five minutes. Under the terrible pressure, she collapsed completely.*

2 Writing description

1 a description
  b action
  c description
  d description
  e action
2 a *lonely*
  b *bleary*
  c *sadly*
  d *gloom*
  e The old man is lonely and unhappy and his surroundings are miserable.
3 a *steadily*
  b The adverb is used to create the impression that the rain is here to stay.
4 *slowly, painfully*
5 The old man's face is compared to a cobweb.
6 The rain on the window pane is compared to tears on unhappy cheeks.

3 Verb forms

1 *locked, brings, appears, think, smashed*
2 *to lock, to bring, to appear, to think, to smash*
3 *I go, I went, I will go; I bring, I brought, I will bring; I have, I had, I will have; I begin, I began, I will begin*
4 The modal verbs followed by the main verbs are: *will come, might help, can see, could buy, would wait*

4 Point of view

1 a *children of the well to do, wealthy children, The rich kids, spoilt brats, unbearably spoilt brats*
  b The chain suggests that the author dislikes the children she describes very much.
  c It seems Penny Boynton is being a little unfair. She is judging all the children in exactly the same way. They surely cannot *all* have been that bad!
2 The verbs suggest that the children are not doing anything at all very serious. Boynton is indicating that the children are wasting their time on unimportant things.

3 *In their early days*
4 a *They catered only for children of the well to do in their early days.*
  b She avoided starting both the second and the third sentence with the word *They*. It would have been a little clumsy to have done this.
5 *now*
6 a *Stage schools, They, centres of excellence, They*
  b She now describes them as wonderful.
7 The adjectives are: *constructive, stimulating, excellent*
8 The determiners (*all* and *every*) suggest that now *all* children can benefit from stage school, not just the privileged few.

5 Participles

1 *talked, thought, bought, grown, swum*
2 a *I have thought about it. She has done very well. They have made up their minds.*
  b *I had thought about it. She had done very well. They had made up their minds.*
3 *I had brought my coat in case it rained. The baby is crying because he has hurt himself. He was washing up before she had finished.*
4 *cramped, fallen, tried, tested, spun*

6 Fact and opinion

1 a The Open Day will be on Tuesday, 6th April and will start at 9.30.
  b The Open Day will start off in Room P4.
2 Tim believes people will have an *excellent* day.
3 A modal verb is used in this way in the first sentence.
4 *exhibitions of students' work, demonstrations of activities, chances for parents, a variety of events, introduction from Mrs Cooke*
5 a *We do hope you will be able to attend.*
  b He is trying to make his audience feel as welcome as possible. He is trying to encourage as many people to come as he can.
6 *It's going to be an excellent day.*

7 Using connectives

1 a *Arun, Harry, I*
  b *think, made, flies, have, collect*
  c *tea, planes, fun, fossils*
2 The sentences should be similar to these: *Sid cooks dinner unless his mum does it for him. He makes the toast while his eggs are boiling. He washes up because nobody else will do it for him. He cleans his teeth as/while he watches the television.*

3 a *Having waved to the crowds, the president returned to his office. Having beaten the egg, he poured it into the mixer. Having spoken to the press, Kirsty went back to her hotel.*

  b *After waving to the crowds, the president returned to his office. After beating the egg, he poured it into the mixer. After speaking to the press, Kirsty went back to her hotel.*

8 Literary writing

1 Donleavy is chewing a blade of grass and Farrell is creeping around in oversized shorts. Donleavy is completely relaxed and Farrell is terrified.

2 a Donleavy tells Farrell politely.

  b Farrell is rude to Donleavy. He tells him to 'get lost'.

  c Donleavy's friends pretend to be offended by Farrell's rudeness.

3 a Donleavy speaks patiently to Farrell, as if trying to explain something difficult to him.

  b Donleavy pretends that punishing Farrell will make him feel sad.

4 *hangers on, parasites*

5 a Donleavy's friends always laugh loudest at his jokes.

  b The narrator believes his jokes are 'nasty'.

6 a *sidled*

  b *froze*

7 *grabbed, wrenched*

9 Foregrounds in sentences

1 *In a second, he'll be coming. In a fury, she strode off. On a lonely hilltop, he lay down silently.*

2 The sentences should be similar to these: *Unhappily, they parted for the last time. Eagerly, the children ran into the fairground.*

3 *If you don't stop messing around, I'm going to lose my temper. When she found out, it was a real problem. Until the next time, take care.*

4 *Laughing all the time, he watched the film. Crying loudly, the baby woke me. Breathing deeply, she prepared her performance.*

5 The foregrounded features (in sentence order) are: a participle phrase, an adverb, an adverbial phrase

10 Features of narrative

1 *early, during the night, already, after a while, in the end*

2 *finally*

3 The first anecdote is about the collapse of Tent 3. The second anecdote is about the teacher burning the sausages.

4 a The first anecdote is made amusing by the way the girls use the tent as a duvet.

  b The second anecdote is made funny because the teacher blames the cooker but everyone knows it is his fault.

5 a *out of date*

  b They probably believe Mr Walters cannot cook.

6 *We believed you, Mr Walters.*

7 *nobody minded at all*

11 Using adjectives

1 The people are *angry* and *frustrated*. The proposal is *absurd.* The park (and its trees) are *magnificent* and *wonderful*.

2 *people*

3 *the grim, dark night/the grim and dark night; the quiet volcano; the hot, spicy curry/the hot and spicy curry*

4 The sentences should be similar to these: *The large aeroplane sped through the sky. The luxury yacht sped through the waves.*

5 a *Our magnificent park with its wonderful trees*

  b *with*

12 Creating mood

1 a *dusty*

  b They are always in the same order.

  c The writer suggests that these books are never read or even moved.

2 a *a lonely spider plant; some crumpled, glossy magazines*

  b *lonely, crumpled*

3 *sadly*

4 *drooped*

5 a *shiny, fantastic*

  b *beaming*

  c The real world of the waiting room is dusty and gloomy. This contrasts with the make-believe world which is shiny and happy.

6 *There was a lonely spider plant that drooped down sadly above them./A lonely spider plant that drooped down sadly was above them.*

13 Test 1

1 *mask, occasion, surprise, key, planet*

2 a *pear, costs, students, friends, plant*

  b *spiralling, eager, lonely*

  c *some, my, the*

3 a *a web, the dark corner, my uncle, some relations, that excellent café, the crossroads*

  b *in, with, at*

4 a *waited, disappeared, work*

  b *under, in, during*

  c *Under the winter snow, the seed waited. In a desperate panic, Jake disappeared. During daylight, I work.*

5 *simile*

6 a *should, might, may, can, could*
   b *be, get, calm, speak, put*
7 a *Fruit flies, These infuriating creatures, They, They, They, insect vermin*
   b *They*
   c The writer dislikes fruit flies in a very intense and passionate way.
8 a *He has swum for us. They have broken their promises.*
   b *He had swum for us. They had broken their promises.*
   c *He is swimming for us. They are breaking their promises.*
   d *He was swimming for us. They were breaking their promises.*
9 The verb *do* is often placed before a main verb for emphasis. For example, *I **do** make my own bed.*
10 The sentences should be similar to these: *Mark went straight home after he had left our house. Bring something to eat if you want to come with us. They were still in the park when the downpour started.* You may have chosen different connectives that still make perfectly good sense.

14 Formal and informal

1 a *Hi guys*
   b exclamation mark
   c *whooeee*
2 *Sorry not to have been in touch for so long.*
3 a *I'm, here's*
   b *I am, here is*
4 *next, now*
5 *Press down firmly with both hands. Next, push the rockers into place.*

15 Explanations

1 a at junior school
   b the Saxons and the Romans
   c epidemics, witch hunts and famines
2 a *love, were* (*were* is a past tense form of the verb *be*)
   b The first verb is in the (simple) present tense and the second is in the (simple) past.
   c In the first sentence, the writer is describing the way she feels now. In the second sentence, she is explaining the way people were in the past.
3 a She says there are no women teachers and that history is full of men.
   b *the first reason, the second reason*
   c Some of her friends
   d *definitely*
4 *The second reason is more important, though.*
5 *Think about it.*
6 She calls historical men *superheroes* and she uses an exclamation mark too.

16 Features of argument

1 The writer suggests that interest is growing in the five-term year.
2 *many schools*
3 a *many schools around the country*
   b They show that it is not just schools that are known to the writer locally. It is schools all over the place that are thinking like this.
4 a *some progressive schools*
   b The adjective suggests that in adopting the five-term year these schools are forward looking.
5 a *outdated; three-term*
   b It suggests she would like to get rid of the three-term year.
6 She is suggesting that schools with a five-term year are ahead of the game. The schools that do not have it are lagging behind.

17 Punctuating sentences

1 a the soldier
   b a rat
2 *The scout, She, The merry barber with the wide grin*
3 a *his knife*
   b *everyone's equipment*
   c *his ankle*
   d *down the trench*
4 The writer separates the clauses with commas.
5 *The soldier sharpened his knife as he walked down the trench. As he walked down the trench, the soldier sharpened his knife. Walking down the trench, the soldier sharpened his knife.*

18 Literary verse

1 a *crag*
   b *Close to the sun*
2 a *wrinkled*
   b *crawls*
3 The description of the sea suggests that the eagle is a long way away from it.
4 a *clasps, crag, crooked, close, crawls*
   b *crooked*
   c Tennyson may have wanted to emphasise the harsh, cruel, hard world in which the eagle lives.
5 a The simile makes the claws seem sharp and more dangerous. They are like weapons.
   b The eagle falls like *a thunderbolt*.
   c The simile suggests that the eagle has great speed and strength.
6 The poet uses the word *hands* to make the eagle seem more human.
7 a The eagle is sitting perfectly still and waiting. This creates an atmosphere of suspense, since the reader knows the eagle must be waiting *for* something.

b *He watches*

c The eagle might be dropping down to catch some form of prey.

19 Using adverbs

1 *The work progressed slowly. Music was played loudly.*

2 *yesterday, now, again, soon, then*

3 *Come in/Come over, Go through/Go outside/Go in, look underneath.*

4 *totally, rather, incredibly, just, too, very*

5 *Come here. The crowd disappeared instantly. Yours is next.*

6 *Constantly, he thought about it. He constantly thought about it. He thought constantly about it. He thought about it constantly.*

20 Persuasive techniques

1 a *you*

b It makes the reader feel singled out. It is as if the writer is talking directly to the reader.

2 a There are three rhetorical questions in this extract.

b Most people would wish to answer these questions with a *yes.*

c The writer hopes this will have the effect of making readers answer *yes* to the final question as well.

3 a Helpers are made to feel that they will not be giving up *too* much of their own time.

b The second phrase shows that the writer understands time is valuable to people. It is as if people own the time that they are donating to the fair.

c The third phrase shows that the effort made by volunteers is for something worthwhile.

4 *enthusiastic, energetic*

5 a *we are looking for*

b *We need*

c *help*

6 a *our*

b It suggests that the writer feels proud of it. It is something that belongs to the writer but which the writer clearly wants to share.

21 Range of perspectives

1 a *many people*

b *teenagers*

c *toddlers*

d *mums and dads*

e *some people*

f *the writer (I)*

g The text conveys six different points of view.

2 a bored

b Some of them respond to these feelings by becoming involved in crime.

c They would have the existing play area all to themselves.

d They wouldn't have to worry so much about their children being hurt or knocked over.

3 a *I feel strongly*

b *think*

c *believe*

4 a The writer is asking the readers of the letter (the local council) to *consider the toddlers.*

b The council's viewpoint is important because it is the councillors who will be making the decision as to whether or not to build the skateboard park.

5 *nowhere to go, don't have anywhere else to go*

22 Structuring sentences

1 *I, Beach fashions, The enormous crocodile*

2 *is running, has seemed, blows*

3 *at the corner, all night long, quietly*

4 There are many ways in which you could develop this sentence. The noun phrase to replace *She* could be *The old woman* or *The young girl.* The verb *murmured* could be lengthened by *is murmuring* or *has been murmuring.* The adverbial could be developed as *quietly to herself* or *quietly in the kitchen.* An example of a sentence expanded within the same structure would be: *The old woman has been murmuring quietly to herself in the kitchen.*

23 What if?

1 *It seems likely that aliens crashed into New Mexico on June 12th 1957.*

2 a This creates a much more definite and certain statement.

b The writer included the four words because he didn't want to commit himself to such a certain statement.

3 The adjective *probable* is used in the text as the adverb *probably.*

4 a The *if* statement expresses the possibility that the aliens are still alive.

b The *then* statement suggests that the aliens are being held captive beneath the desert.

5 a *would, might*

b *to be*

6 a The modal in the penultimate sentence expresses certainty.

b This is because he is sure that an interview with an alien would be a dream for most people reading his article.

24 Spelling homophones

1 *flower, waste, threw, night, write, peace*
2 a *place* or *situation*
   b *here*
3 *They're driving over now. Here comes the bus. He doesn't know where it is. They like their new house. I can't hear you very well. They're not doing it properly. Did he wear a tie? Sit over there. There's a problem. The problem is theirs.*
4 All the uses of *its/it's* are incorrect.

25 Shakespeare

1 a An Egyptian charmer gave Othello's mother the handkerchief.
   b Othello's mother gave him the handkerchief when she was dying.
   c She told him to give the handkerchief to his wife when he married.
2 a The clairvoyant could almost read people's thoughts.
   b The handkerchief would make Othello's mother appear desirable. The word in the text, *amiable*, now means just good natured and friendly. Its meaning has changed since Shakespeare's time.
   c His spirits would hunt after 'new fancies'. In other words, he would look for other women.
3 He asks Desdemona to make the handkerchief her darling.
4 a Othello's father's eye is referred to first.
   b His father's eye would hold his mother 'loathly'.
   c He uses the adjective 'precious'.
   d He believes they will all go to hell.
5 Othello seems extremely superstitious. He makes a lot of the omens and predictions surrounding the handkerchief and what might happen if it were lost. He is being very hard on Desdemona as well. After all, she didn't intend to lose his handkerchief.

6 *An Egyptian gave that handkerchief to my mother.*
7 Nowadays the word is used to describe someone who is charming (perhaps even falsely charming).
8 Othello describes the action of getting married (to a wife).
9 *loathe*
10 *It would, on it*

26 Test 2

1 *Under the earth, there are many life forms.*
   Into the dark night, she vanished.
   Around eight o'clock, the beach changes completely.
2 Possible answers are: *This noisy/excited/angry crowd, Many broken windows, The crashing/thundering waterfall*
3 Possible answers are: *The building appears old/dangerous, These forests are beautiful/endangered, That old metal has gone rusty*
4 *The small boy, She, Oranges, The Power Rangers costume*
5 *is sharpening, smiled, are, will be arriving*
6 *she went, all her friends smiled, she chatted*
7 *through the mall* – prepositional, *into her favourite café* – prepositional, *at her* – adverbial, *to them* – adverbial
8 *Martha walked through the mall. She went into her favourite café. All her friends smiled at her. She chatted to them.*
9 *Instantly, Euan changed his mind. Euan instantly changed his mind. Euan changed his mind instantly.*
10 The first sentence is all correct. In the other sentences, the corrected words are: *it's, They're, its, you're, there*

Revision notes